The Seven Major Chakras

Keeping It Simple

Joan S. Peck

The Seven Major Chakras: Keeping It Simple
by Joan S. Peck

Copyright © 2009 Joan Peck
ISBN: 978-0-9824607-3-3
First Edition: April 2009

Published by:
BEJEWELED PRESS
Phone: 702-699-8183
Website: www.bejeweledpress.com

All rights reserved. No part of this book may be reproduced or transmitted in any form or by any means, electronic or mechanical, including photocopying, recording or by any information storage and retrieval system without written permission from the publisher. Portions of this book may be freely quoted for review purposes up to 500 words, provided credit is given to the source.

The intent of this material is to provide general information to help your quest for emotional and spiritual growth. The author and publisher of this book do not dispense medical advice or prescribe any technique as a form of treatment for physical or emotional problems and therefore assume no responsibility for your actions.

Printed in the United States of America

Table of Contents

Dedication iv
Acknowledgements v
Preface vi
One: Brief History of Chakras 1
Two: First Chakra - Root 3
Three: Second Chakra – Belly (Sacral) 5
Four: Third Chakra – Solar Plexus 7
Five: Fourth Chakra – Heart 9
Six: Fifth Chakra – Throat 11
Seven: Sixth Chakra – Third Eye 13
Eight: Seventh Chakra – Crown 15
Nine: Discovering Your Own Dominant Chakra(s) ... 17
Ten: Healing Colors and Essential Oils for Each Chakra . 24
Eleven: How to Care and Cleanse Crystals 30
Twelve: Simple Meditations to Balance the Chakras 34
Thirteen: Your Own Practice Workbook 38
Bibliography 45
Notes 46
About the Author 50

Dedication

This book is dedicated to my three children:
My daughters Jennifer and Shelly, and my
son, Jay, who died in 2005.

You three are the best part of me.

Acknowledgements

First and foremost, I want to thank all the authors who are listed in my Bibliography. Much of my book is their work that I have gathered for my primer, *The Seven Major Chakras – Keeping it Simple.* They humble me with all their detail and knowledge; I am forever grateful to them.

I have been so blessed throughout my life with friends who are kindred spirits, who have been there for me, encouraging me to stretch and grow. I send each of you blessings; you know who you are. Know, too, that I feel blessed having you in my life; you are my living angels.

I was so pleased to meet Tony Stubbs, an author in his own right of many books that continue to be read, especially his *An Ascension Handbook.* I am forever appreciative that Tony, as my editor, has taken this inexperienced author and helped her step-by-step on how to get a book published.

I am proud to have shared my book with those who have acknowledged their reading of it with positive comments that you find on the back cover. Each of these professionals has accomplished much spiritually and I am honored to call them friends.

And so we begin another journey together ...

Preface

I relate growing up in the late 1940s and in the 1950s as a time period of little independent thought or to be more accurate a time period of following "the rules" – society's rules, that is. It was after the war had ended and people were happy to have it over and done with, and their men back home, ready to get back to the schedules that made us all feel secure. Along with that came the return of the woman's "duties" that were taught and touted in school books in home economic classes and sometimes reaffirmed in church classes. One of the school books we used in our Home EC class instructed us that, as wives, we had a duty to get dressed up, put on lipstick and make ourselves presentable for our husbands when they waltzed in the door after a day's work, so that they could have the fine dinner they had earned, along with the attention and service they also deserved.

For many of us of that era, we were taught and expected to fulfill these duties and concentrate on the needs of others, whether it be our husband, children, parents, extended family members, or even acknowledged as the caretaker of the family pet, the dog's mother! Although the intentions may have been good, much of this type of teaching and expectations left many of us confused and lost. Was this really our role in life? Were our only choices to be a wife, teacher, secretary or nurse? Why did I feel so unfulfilled?

I would periodically think back on the time in my life that as a child I had choked and couldn't catch my breath, and thought that I was going to die. I clearly remember the bright light, bells ringing, beautiful music and bright, bright colors. I also remember the sense of peace and calm that came over me and it was almost disappointing to have my neighbor whack me repeatedly on the back until I could catch my breath. I had raked in air while trying to breathe and it had made me hoarse for several days ... a constant reminder that I'd had a glimpse of something greater, something more. So what did it mean? Why did I always carry this image with me and pull it out whenever I felt low or unhappy?

I was in an unhappy, abusive marriage that involved our three children. Things just didn't make sense to me. Life was nowhere near the "... and they lived happily ever after." So I started to seek out people to better understand life in the spiritual sense. I began to grasp that I was on my own journey, that life itself was a journey. I learned we are all one and that the most important thing in life is love. Love of all kinds, not just between a man and a woman, not just sexual love. Knowing this, however, didn't help me much when the one love I most struggled with was love of my body and appreciation for who I was.

Women, in general, have a hard time not seeing their own beauty if it differs from what models look like. We are also taught 'if you look good, you will feel good.' We all know that is not necessarily so. The thing that made me want to push myself to look at all of this in a different light was when I was told, "You have a responsibility to take care of the body God gave you!" That surely did it for me. After all, I had grown up with duty and responsibility, so that statement was a very comfortable one for me and I felt, if not excited, certainly obliged to move ahead.

As I began to explore the spiritual aspects of various teachings such as Taoism, read Joseph Campbell, and many various self-help books, I came across the energy cycles of our body, Chakras. I have never been good at history, a subject I found boring when it was reduced to dates and one line occurrences. But the history of people who as early as

2,000 B.C.E. understood their bodies as differing speeds of energy fascinated me. The more I looked at the past in this way, the more it became the present or timeless to me. It all began to make sense. And I became overjoyed with what I was discovering. The more that I read about the chakras, the more I thought back on the time when I was a child and was choking. If all the chakras are in alignment, then the seventh chakra, the crown can open and connect you with your consciousness. Your basic life force is open. If that was what had happened to me, then I'd like that sense of well being again and again.

I began to read more and more about chakras until I became overwhelmed. Just too much information. I kept thinking: *There has to be a way to gather all of this information in an easy format, something simple. It shouldn't be so confusing to read about the basic understanding of the chakras, how aligning these energies can help heal the body, how crystals can aid in that and the ultimate goal of opening up your crown chakra to commune with your higher power.*

So after many hours of weeding through information, I offer you, with great enthusiasm and humility, my version of the seven main wheels of life and the important aspects and effects surrounding them.

As you will learn, each of the seven chakras has its own color, and together form the colors of the rainbow. So as we begin to explore the chakras, may each one of us, both female and male, learn to recognize ourselves for what we are "jewels of the universe," and to use that for the betterment of self and mankind.

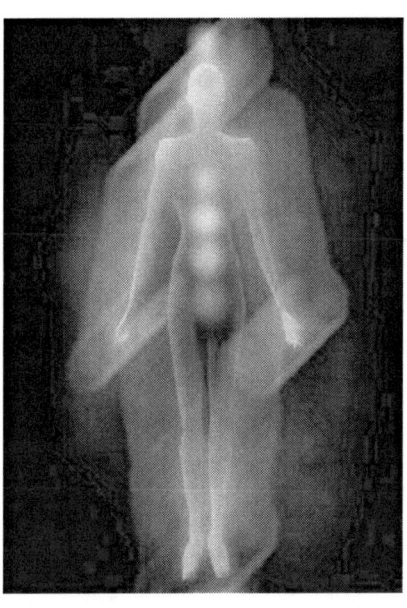

CHAPTER ONE: BRIEF HISTORY OF THE SEVEN MAJOR CHAKRAS

The word "chakra" is derived from the Sanskrit word meaning "wheel" or "disk." It is often described by psychics or clairvoyants as a spinning wheel of colorful light. The chakras begin at the base of the spine and finish over the top of the head. Although they are fixed in the central spinal column, they are located both in the front and the back of the body, and work through it.

Each chakra has a different color and vibrates and rotates at a different speed. The first chakra, the Root rotates at the slowest speed, and the seventh or crown, at the highest speed. The size and brightness of the wheels vary with individual development, physical condition, energy levels, disease, or stress. When balanced, the seven chakras help us maintain health, are vehicles to personal empowerment, and connect us to the divine.

Chakras are first mentioned in the Vedas, ancient Hindu scriptures. It is difficult to put a date on the Vedas because they are assumed to have been passed down orally for nearly a thousand years before they were first written down between 1200 and 900 B.C.E.

Later, in the 7th century B.C.E., the main message was that enlightenment (and even immortality) can be achieved by meditating with the awareness that your soul is at one with all creation. Newer texts also explored the concept of karma and reincarnation.

The understanding of the chakras was popularized by Sir John Woodroffe, who wrote under the pseudonym Arthur Avalon, in a book entitled *The Serpent Power – The Secrets of Tantric and Shaktic Yoga*, first published in 1919. This is a guide to kundalini practice (the raising of the energy that lies dormant at the Base Chakra).

The esteemed Swiss psychologist Carl Jung (1875-1961) did much to develop the Western understanding of kundalni. He presented a seminar on kundalini yoga to the Psychological Club in Zurich in 1932, which has subsequently been recognized as a highly significant moment in the appreciation of Eastern thought by the West.

There is much more to understanding the history of chakras that can be found in various books. Anodea Judith is the leading expert on chakras and her latest book, *Wheels of Life* is excellent, with much greater detail than presented here. Another book, *The Chakra Bible* by Patricia Merier is exceptionally complete in encompassing the history of chakras with their ancient names, the spiritual, emotional and health issues connected to the chakras and much, much more.

As Eastern Ideas were increasingly explored and accepted by the West, particularly through the practice of yoga, there is a greater understanding and appreciation of our life forces, in particular, the chakras. Knowledge is power, and who doesn't like to be empowered? So let's begin.

CHAPTER TWO: FIRST CHAKRA — ROOT

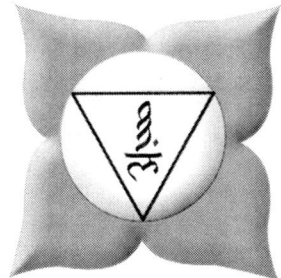

FIRST CHAKRA - ROOT: located at the base of the spine at the tailbone in the back and the pubic bone in front. (Colors used: red, brown, black.)

Root body parts: include hips, legs, feet, lower back and sexual organs.

Element: Earth

Center: Manifestation. When trying to make things happen in the material world, business or material possessions, the energy to succeed will come from the first chakra.

Emotions: Basic needs - primal instinct, survival, security, safety.

Blocked Emotions: fearful, anxious, insecure and frustrated.

Physical Problems: weight problems, hemorrhoids, degenerative arthritis, knee troubles, sciatica.

Gemstones: Garnet, Ruby, Smoky Quartz, Obsidian and Black Tourmaline.

GEMSTONES:
- *Garnet* – speeds up all healing processes. All garnets bring a fiery, warming energy to fight cold, sluggish or damp disease states.
- *Ruby* – balances the heart, both subtly and physically; helps to engender feelings of confidence, security, enthusiasm and self-esteem.
- *Smoky Quartz* – calms the mind and focuses its thoughts; gently grounds us.
- *Obsidian* – as a stone that emerges from the ground with dramatic force is able to bring hidden issues, emotions and traumas to the surface; rebalances the digestive system; grounds and protects us.
- *Black Tourmaline* – realigns the structures of the body; soothes and settles bones and muscles; focuses awareness in the present; strengthens our grip on reality.

Chapter Three: Second Chakra – Belly (Sacral)

Second Chakra – Belly: located 2 inches below the navel (Color used: orange.)

Root body parts: include women's sexual organs, kidneys, bladder and large intestine, circulatory system.

Element: Water

Center: It governs our ability to relate to others in an open and friendly way. It is the vortex of change, emotion, pleasure and movement.

Emotions: Basic needs - sexuality, creativity, intuition, and self-worth.

Blocked Emotions: emotionally explosive, manipulative, obsessed with thoughts of sex or may lack energy.

Physical Problems: kidney weakness, stiff lower back, constipation, and muscle spasms.

Gemstones: Carnelian, Orange Calcite, Coral, Moonstone, Tigers Eye

GEMSTONES:
- *Carnelian* – Releases stress and trauma; enhances creativity; repairs subtle bodies.
- *Orange Calcite* – Releases feelings of stress and impatience; helps with problem-solving; useful for studying and taking exams.
- *Coral* – Strengthens the heart, circulation and bones; balances and steadies the emotions; boosts fertility and our drive to satisfy desires.
- *Moonstone* – balances the body's blood and lymph systems; relieves menstrual cramps and helps with other female issues; relieves indigestion; enhances intuition and imagination.
- *Tigers Eye* – soothes both physically and mentally; builds confidence; encourages contact with other people.

Chapter Four: Third Chakra — Solar Plexus

Third Chakra - Solar Plexus: located 2 inches below the breastbone in the center behind the stomach (Color used: yellow.)

Root body parts: include stomach, liver, gall bladder, pancreas, digestive system and small intestine.

Element: Fire

Center: Transformation, center of personal power and strength. It is also the center for astral travel and astral influences, receptivity of spirit guides and psychic development.

Emotions: Self-esteem, anger, ego, passions, impulses, mental acuity

Blocked Emotions: Lack of confidence, confusion, worry about what others think, feeling that others are controlling your life, depressed.

Physical Problems: Digestive difficulties, liver problems, diabetes, nervous exhaustion, and food allergies.

Gemstones: Citrine, Topaz, Amber and Yellow Calcite

GEMSTONES:
- *Citrine* – anchors and activates the lower chakras; is restful and warming; boosts confidence and creates a sense of personal power; provides a "sunny" energy to stimulate the mind in the winter months.

- *Topaz* – releases physical tension; helps to stabilize the emotions; increases motivation and confidence; harmonizes all layers of subtle energy.

- *Amber* – invigorates the body's systems; helps with nervous disorders; boosts energy and generates enthusiasm; sharpens thinking processes.

- *Yellow Calcite* – shifts energy that has become stagnant or very slow-moving; sooths and calms agitated emotions; quiets the mind; creates clarity by removing friction and dissonance.

Chapter Five: Fourth Chakra – Heart

Fourth Chakra - Heart: located behind breast bone in front and on the spine between the shoulder blades in back. (Color used: green and pink.)

Root body parts: include heart, lungs, circulatory system, thymus, arms, hands, shoulders and upper back.

Element: Air

Center: Balance and healing, spirituality and unity. This is the chakra that connects body and mind with spirit. This center directs one's ability to love themselves and others, to give and to receive love.

Emotions: Love, compassion, healing and spirituality

Blocked Emotions: May feel sorry for self, paranoid, indecisive, afraid of letting go, afraid of getting hurt or unworthy of love.

Physical Problems: asthma, high blood pressure, heart disease, lung disease, insomnia and difficulty in breathing.

Gemstones: Rose Quartz, Kunzite, Emerald, Jade, and Watermelon Tourmaline

GEMSTONES:
- *Rose Quartz* – rapidly releases emotional stress – the effect is so intense that it can be uncomfortable (to avoid this, balance with grounding stones); uncovers the underlying causes of other problems, such as a negative self-esteem.
- *Kunzite* – Supports the cardiovascular system and thyroid function; enhances self-esteem; helps to override negative, unhelpful thought patterns – very protective; creates a space for meditation.
- *Emerald* – speeds cleansing and purifying processes; assuages hidden fears and anxieties; effective as a focus for meditation.
- *Jade* – balances the heart chakra, which helps to improve our relationships with other people; increases a sense of belonging; enhances the ability to act appropriately and effectively; relaxes us on a deep level, helping to heal.
- *Watermelon Tourmaline* – excellent for balancing the heart chakra on all levels.

Chapter Six: Fifth Chakra – Throat

Fifth Chakra – Throat: located in the V of the collarbone at the lower neck. (Color used: light blue.)

Root body parts: include the throat, neck, teeth, ears, and thyroid gland.

Element: Sound

Center: Center of communication, sound and expression of creativity via thought, speech and writing. The possibility of change, transformation and healing are located. Anger is stored in the throat.

Emotions: Self-expression, speech

Blocked Emotions: Angry, feel timid, be quiet, feel weak or can't express your thoughts.

Physical Problems: Sore throat, stiff neck, hearing problems, thyroid problems, cold, skin irritations, ear infections and back pain.

Gemstones: Aquamarine, Azurite, Celestite, Turquoise

GEMSTONES:
- *Aquamarine* – boosts the immune system, balances the thymus and throat chakras; clears stagnant emotions; encourages optimism; enables creative expression of ideas; encourages unique skills; helps to find inspiration.
- *Azurite* – accesses deep levels of body consciousness; draws out memories or old stress, allowing them to be released in healing; improves communication and creative flow.
- *Celestite* – encourages communication and expression; helps to lighten our mood when needed; opens the mind to new ideas; encourages blissful silence, inspiration, meditative states and heightened intuition.
- *Turquoise* – strengthens all organs; balances all the subtle systems, particularly the heart, thymus and throat chakras; neutralizes environmental negativity; cools emotions; calms overactive thoughts; enhances intuition and psychic skills.

Chapter Seven: Sixth Chakra – Third Eye

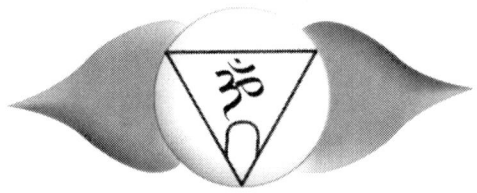

Sixth Chakra – Third Eye located above the physical eyes on the center of the forehead. (Colors used: purple and dark blue)

Root body parts: include eyes, face, brain, lymphatic and endocrine system.

Element: Light

Center: Intuition, imagination, visualization, clairvoyance and vision. It assists in the purification of negative tendencies and in the elimination of selfish attitudes. Through the power of the sixth chakra, you can receive guidance, channel and tune into your Higher Self.

Emotions: Intuition, extra sensory perception

Blocked Emotions: Non-assertive, afraid of success, or be egotistical

Physical Problems: Headaches, blurred vision, blindness and eyestrain.

Gemstones: Amethyst, Sodalite, Star Sapphire and Lapis Lazuli

GEMSTONES:
- *Amethyst* – encourages self-control; calms harsh emotions and brings stability; helps practical applications of imagination; aids meditation and sleep.
- *Sodalite* – cleanses the lymphatic system, enhancing the immune system; stabilizes emotions; clarifies perception; expands awareness during meditation; encourages peace and contentment.
- *Star Sapphire* – balances the endocrine system and reins in overactive energies; calms, regulates and reduces tension in the solar plexus created by fear and anxiety; increases power of personal expression, benefiting the heart and throat chakras; stimulates the higher mind.
- *Lapis Lazuli* – supports the throat and upper chest areas; draws anxieties to the surface; aids communication and meditation; provides insight and clarity of mind.

Chapter Eight: Seventh Chakra – Crown

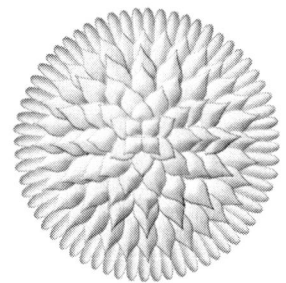

Seventh Chakra – Crown located just behind the top of the skull. (Colors used: white and purple)

Root body parts: None.

Element: Thought

Center: Consciousness and transcendence. The center of spirituality, enlightenment, dynamic thought and energy. It allows for the inward flow of wisdom and connectedness with God, the place where life animates the physical body.

Emotions: Divinity, peace, enlightenment

Blocked Emotions: Sense of frustration, no spark of joy, destructive feelings.

Physical Problems: migraine headaches, depression, inability to learn, confusion, apathy, alienation, boredom.

Gemstones: Clear Quartz Crystal, Oregon Opal, Diamond and Amethyst

GEMSTONES:
- *Clear Quartz Crystal* – amplifies and strengthens the whole aura; cleanses and shifts energy; releases blocked emotions and helps to bring about calm; increases clarity of thought and sharpness of perception; brings spiritual peace, ideal for meditation and contemplation.
- *Oregon Opal* – stabilizes the emotions; increases sense of self-worth; energizes the crown chakra.
- *Diamond* – rebalances the skull, jaw and spine; acts as a powerful detoxifier on all levels – so powerful that you may need to use other calming stones to modify its action; removes negativity and emotional blocks; transforms sluggish and mundane thought processes to a broader, universal view; supports meditation and spiritual ventures.
- *Amethyst* – encourages self-control; calms harsh emotions and brings stability; helps practical applications of imagination; aids meditation and sleep.

Chapter Nine: Discovering Your Own Dominant Chakras

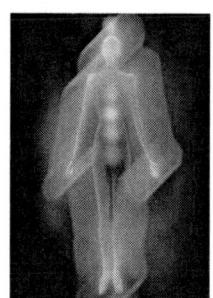

What Are Your Dominant Chakras?

"Healing With Crystals & Chakra Energies" by Sue and Simon Lilly

1. Which area(s) of your body concern you the most?
    1. feet and hands
    2. between the waist and hips
    3. waist
    4. chest
    5. neck and shoulders
    6. face
    7. head

2. Which area(s) of your body do you dislike?
    1. feet and hands
    2. between the waist and hips
    3. waist
    4. chest
    5. neck and shoulders
    6. face
    7. head

3. Which area(s) of your body are you proud of?
    1. feet and hands
    2. between the waist and the hips
    3. waist
    4. chest
    5. neck and shoulders
    6. face
    7. head

4. Which area(s) of your body are affected by major health issues?
    1. feet
    2. between the waist and hips
    3. waist
    4. chest
    5. neck and shoulders
    6. face
    7. head

5. Which area(s) are affected most by minor health issues?
    1. feet
    2. between the waist and hips
    3. waist
    4. chest
    5. neck and shoulders
    6. face
    7. head

6. Which color(s) do you like the most?
    1. red
    2. orange
    3. yellow
    4. green

5. blue
6. dark blue
7. violet

7. Which color(s) do you like the least?
    1. red
    2. orange
    3. yellow
    4. green
    5. blue
    6. dark blue
    7. violet

8. Which are your favorite foods?
    1. meat/fish
    2. rice/orange fruits
    3. wheat/yellow fruits
    4. green fruit and vegetables

9. Which kind of exercises or interests attract you?
    1. fast action
    2. dancing/painting
    3. crosswords/puzzles
    4. anything outside
    5. drama/singing
    6. mystery/crime novels
    7. doing nothing

10. What sort of people do you look up to and admire?
    1. sportspeople
    2. artists/musicians
    3. intellectuals
    4. conservationists

5. speakers/politicians
6. inventors
7. mystics/religious figures

11. What sort of person do you think of yourself as?
    1. get on with things
    2. creative
    3. thinker/worrier
    4. emotional
    5. chatterbox
    6. quiet
    7. daydreamer

12. What emotions do you consider are uppermost in your life?
    1. passionate
    2. easy-going
    3. contented
    4. caring, sharing
    5. loyal
    6. helpfully distant
    7. sympathetic

13. What emotions do you have that you would like to change?
    1. temper
    2. possessiveness
    3. confusion
    4. insecurity
    5. needing things to be "black or white"
    6. feeling separate from others
    7. not saying "no"

14. If you get angry, what is your most common reaction?
    1. rage/tantrums
    2. sullen resentment
    3. get frightened
    4. blame yourself
    5. keep quiet
    6. withdraw
    7. imagine nothing happened

15. What are you most afraid of?
    1. dying
    2. lack of sensation
    3. things you don't understand
    4. being alone
    5. having no one to talk to
    6. losing your way
    7. difficult situations

16. Which of these describes the way you prefer to learn?
    1. fast
    2. slowly
    3. quickly but forget
    4. through feelings
    5. by rote
    6. instinctively
    7. can't be bothered

17. What best describes your reaction to situations?
    1. enthusiastic
    2. go with the flow
    3. think things through
    4. see how things feel

5. ask a lot of questions
   6. see the patterns then act
   7. drift along

18. If you are criticized or reprimanded, what is your usual response?
    1. anger
    2. resentment
    3. fear
    4. self-blame
    5. verbal retort
    6. think about it
    7. denial

19. How would you describe your favorite books, films, video games?
    1. combat action
    2. art
    3. skill, intellectual
    4. romances
    5. courtroom dramas
    6. detective stories
    7. spiritual or self development

20. Which category best describes your friends?
    1. competitive
    2. creative
    3. intellectual
    4. loving
    5. idealistic
    6. rebellious
    7. spiritual

Questionnaire Assessment

When you have completed answering the questions, count how many times you have circled each of the seven numbers. The numbers used in the answers to the questions correlate with the chakras and the number(s) you have circled the most indicates what chakra(s) are dominant for you.

Since you want to keep all your chakras in balance, concentrate on your dominant chakra(s) to see what is going on in your life to make that chakra(s) dominant for you and what steps you can take to bring it into a cleared state if it is blocked and to ensure that all your chakras are in balance and open to the crown.

CHAPTER TEN: HEALING COLORS AND ESSENTIAL OILS FOR EACH CHAKRA

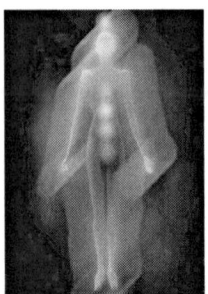

QUALITIES OF DIFFERENT-COLORED LIGHTS

From the Chakra Bible by Patricia Mercier

RED light is stimulating, in particular increasing energy to aid blood circulation. It is not used if there is anxiety or emotional disturbances – here the complementary turquoise is best.

ORANGE light aids the action of the Sacral Chakra and spleen, where prana is split up into all the colors of the spectrum and flows to the other chakras. It is also used to treat imbalances of energy in the kidneys.

YELLOW light represents the intellect and solar energy. Nerves become activated with yellow, and for this reason it is used to stimulate energy flow through them and through the muscles. It also benefits the skin and plays a part in the energetic metabolism of calcium.

GREEN light is regarded as a cleansing/detoxing color. It is used for all manner of imbalances in the physical body and acts like an antiseptic.

TURQUOISE light, in combination with its complementary red, helps clear the energy of acute infections.

BLUE light is calming; it therefore reduces pain, can enhance spiritual growth and balance sleep patterns.

VIOLET light is appropriate for the eyes and the stagnating energy of nerve-related problems. Violet in the aura indicates inspiration, insight and development of one's higher self or spiritual attainment.

MAGENTA light, used in color therapy, is really only attainable with light, not pigment or dye. Just below the frequency of ultraviolet it can be seen as a soft glow at sunset. Magenta light activates additional chakras above the crown. At bio-energetic level it releases imbalances that can manifest as serious disease. At an emotional level it allows us to let go of old relationships; on a physical level, it helps us to clear out "clutter" from our lives.

Put Colors in Your Life When ...

From Healing with Crystals and Chakra Energies by Sue and Simon Lilly

Put RED into your life when you experience ...
- Lack of enthusiasm and interest.
- Lack of energy and a feeling of over-tiredness.
- An inability to make your dreams a practical reality.
- Feelings of insecurity, unwarranted fear, or anxiety.

Put ORANGE into your life when you experience ...
- Feelings of bleakness and boredom, particularly where there is a sense that time is dragging.
- Lack of interest in what is going on around you, even to the degree of disdaining to become involved in any way.
- Resentment of changes in familiar routines and an obsessive need to have things in their 'proper' place.
- Taking oneself too seriously, being unable to see humor and playfulness in life.
- Fear of experiencing pleasure through the senses and of enjoying sensuality.
- An inability to let go of the past. This can be especially apparent after an accident or shock where the mind continually revolves around the issues involved – the "what if ...," and, "If only I had done ___ instead of ___."
- Problems with blocked experiences in life, such as a decease in personal creativity.

Put YELLOW into your life when you experience ...
- Confusion and indecision.
- Fear and anxiety caused by unknown factors leading to nervous and digestive disorders.

- A weak and confused immune system – frequent minor illnesses, intolerances and allergies to foods and other substances.
- Nervous exhaustion, nervous breakdown, 'burn out', panic attacks, hot flushes.
- Poor memory, inability to concentrate or study
- Tendencies to Seasonal Affective Disorder (SAD) or lethargy and depression in dull weather.
- Digestive difficulties, poor absorption of food.

Put GREEN into your life when you experience ...
- Feelings of restriction caused by circumstances such as being housebound or confined.
- A need to let change happen, but also a fear of the unknown.
- Feelings of being trapped by other people's rules and regulations and a need to break rigid patterns.
- A need for new ideas.
- A need for a new state of balance.
- Problems with personal relationships, especially with over-dominance or subservience.
- Negative green tendencies, feelings and emotions, such as envy, jealousy and greed.

Put BLUE in your life when you experience ...
- A need to calm agitated, excitable or chaotic states.
- A need to communicate clearly.
- A need for help with new information or in seeing information in content.
- A need for peace, detachment, solitude and rest.

Put INDIGO in your life when you experience a need to ...
- Focus on personal issues, beliefs and ideas.
- Develop sensitivity to the inner senses and intuition.
- Cool and quiet normal mental processes.
- Relieve physical, mental and emotional pain.
- Assimilate and understand new concepts or philosophies.
- Temporarily relieve and/or remove everyday problems and difficult experiences in life.
- Find space and a period of solitude.

Put VIOLET in your life when you experience a need to ...
- Rebalance life.
- Speed up the natural healing energy of the body.
- Use your imagination in practical ways.
- Integrate new skills into everyday life.
- Remove all sorts of obstacles in life.
- Calm hyperactivity, or energize lethargy or depression.

Appropriate Essential Oils for Chakra Massage

From the Chakra Bible by Patricia Mercier

CHAKRA	Chakra Qualities	Essential Oils
Root	Grounding/stabilizing Earth Energy	Patchouli, myrrh, cedarwood
Sacral	Transmuting Sexual Energy	Sandalwood, Jasmine, rose, ylang-ylang, champaca
Solar Plexus	Transducing solar and pranic energy	Sage, juniper, geranium
Heart	Flow of unconditional love	Rose, melissa, neroli
Throat	Self-expression, communication, will	Chamomile, lavender, rosemary, thyme
Brow	Balancing the higher and lower selves, ESP	Frankincense, basil
Crown	Divine love and super-consciousness	Ylang-ylang, rosewood, linden

CHAPTER ELEVEN: HOW TO CLEANSE AND CARE FOR CRYSTALS

Before we get into the cleansing and care for your crystals, I want to talk about using crystals and what you can hope to gain from doing so. You do not have to believe in spirit worlds to understand and appreciate the energies that exist in crystals and how they can help you heal or heal others. There is some controversy as to whether you should use only clear crystals or the colored stones of the chakras for the greatest effect. Most of us believe that both methods are effective. You can place the stones on or around the body, placing the stones by color and shape to recreate a quality or tone that encourages healing to take place. You can also wear your favorite stones in jewelry or as a talisman enjoying the energy that you receive from it. Don't forget to cleanse it before and after you wear it to eliminate any negative energy. I once again ask you to refer to my bibliography to see what others much more experienced that I am in the proper guidance of using crystals to heal. It is always good to go to a person well-versed and experienced with crystals so that you can learn from them and work with crystals in the proper way.

Here are two cleansing methods for your review. As you can see, they are quite similar and offer many various ways for you to accomplish your goal of cleansing your crystals.

Crystal Cleansing Methods

from *The Chakra Bible* by Patricia Mercer

All hard crystals can safely be cleansed in clear water, or in water with a small amount of salt in it. Then either put them in the sunshine or in the moonlight to energize them. Other cleansing methods to try are: the smoke of incense, flower remedies, sound, meditation, Reiki healing or placing the stones in the earth – ensure that each time you have love in your heart as you handle the crystals.

Then dedicate your crystal. It may be as simple as "May this crystal work only with the power of Unconditional Love and Light for the highest level of good."

Crystal Cleansing Methods

from *The Essential Crystal Handbook* by Simon and Sue Lilly

New stones, if not water-soluble or too fragile, benefit from washing in warm, soapy water to remove dust and grime. All your stones should be energetically cleansed before and after each use. This is because a crystal functions by absorbing energy from its surroundings into its internal structure, where imbalances are corrected. If it is not cleansed, the crystal will become overloaded, which reduces its effectiveness and may cause it to transfer imbalances into the aura. A "clean" crystal feels lighter and looks brighter than an energetically "tired" stone.

- *Running water and sunlight* – hold the stone under running water and visualize imbalances flowing away. Place in sunlight to dry (not suitable for water-soluble crystals, fragile crystals or crystals that fade in the sunlight).
- *Sound* – strike or ring a singing bowl, bell, cymbal or tuning fork near the crystal for efficient energetic cleansing.
- *Incense smoke* – incense has always been used to cleanse and consecrate. Burn some incense and pass the stone several times through the smoke.
- *Salt* – place the crystal in a bowl and cover with dry sea salt. Leave to stand overnight. Avoid placing crystals in slat water as it corrodes the surfaces.
- *Breath* – exhale sharply over the crystal and imagine imbalances being blown away. Repeat several times.
- *Crystal clusters* – place the stone on any larger crystal cluster to restore natural levels of energy.
- *Essense sprays* – spray the stone with a cleansing flower and gem essence.

Caring for Your Crystals

from *The Essential Crystal Handbook* by Simon and Sue Lilly
- Soft stones can be scraped by harder stones, so keep them apart.
- Locate a light, compartmentalized box and pad each section with soft paper (bead holders work beautifully and can be found at Michaels or Jo-Ann's Fabric stores).
- Don't use too large a box; when filled they become heavy.
- Avoid knocking stones together.
- Natural ends of crystals can chip easily, so store and handle with care.
- Avoid exposing crystals to very strong sunlight or sudden changes of temperature – color can fade and fractures appear.
- Avoid placing shaped spheres in direct sunlight; they can focus the sun's rays and cause fire.

CHAPTER TWELVE: SIMPLE MEDITATIONS TO BALANCE THE CHAKRAS

Chakra Meditation

Chakra is a Sanskrit word for Wheel of Light, and the theory is that these chakras rotate and continuously send off vibrations in a healthy human being. An imbalance indicates that an entire system is out of alignment and can cause physical, mental and spiritual problems. How does an imbalance occur? If energy is blocked even in one chakra, energy does not properly flow through the all the chakras. If a chakra is unclear or fuzzy, it may become blocked. What can cause this? Physical illness, stress, a bad diet, environmental toxins, allergies or a lack of physical activity are some of the ways.

As you can see from the above photos, these are two very important positions you can use when you are meditating. When you cross your legs sitting "Indian style," you are aligning your body from the bottom of your spine where the root chakra resides to the top of your head where the crown chakra is. You can then place your hands palms open, thumb connected to your middle finger at the ends of your knees. This position allows you to receive energy and keep the flow throughout your body.

Or you can place both hands together as if you are praying and keeping them chest high allow once again the energy to flow throughout your body from the root chakra to the crown.

Start feeling every part of your body from toe to head. You may experience a wave of thoughts, fear and every emotion. Don't be disturbed by this; you are releasing stress. With practice, these negative feelings and emotions will disappear and you will be able to get into a relaxed state without interfering thoughts.

Candles, particularly colored candles, increase the energy around you just like color therapy and essential oils do. You can also use flowers. Meditation is meant to expand your inner self and allow you to connect with your higher power. It is during meditation that you can ask your questions to the universe; then remain quiet and open to receiving the answers. Oftentimes the answers will not come to you right away, but perhaps later in the day or in your dreams.

If you have a particular chakra or part of the body that needs healing, you need to be relaxed in order to be open to heal and to work on your chakras. Yoga teaches us that breath is a key to relaxation and meditation. It is important to keep to your own rhythm drawing air in through the nose and out through the mouth, relaxing deeper and deeper. Ask the angels of healing to assist you and become a channel for them.

Balancing your chakras is a form of self-healing. Another way for you to get your chakras in alignment is to go to a healer who performs Reiki. Make sure that you get references and that they are legitimately a Reiki Master. These healers work with your body to shift and move your energy around so that all your chakras are in balance.

Also, I highly recommend reading as much information as possible regarding the chakras. Most notably, study Anodea Judith's books. I list those and other worthy books in my bibliography.

Following are several meditations you can do yourself to help keep all of your chakras in balance. One of my favorites one is by Mike from the website www.crystallinks.com.

Mike's Meditation

Prepare as you would for meditation. Close your eyes. Visualize your left hand holding balloons on strings, each one a different color – the colors of the chakras – plus one pink balloon. Next, visualize the red balloon moving across your field of vision from left to right. Let go of the string and focus on the balloon as it floats up and out of sight. Next, visualize the orange balloon floating in the same pattern as the red one took. Continue with each color until all that is left is the pink balloon which moves across your field of vision until it too floats away as far as your consciousness can travel. Allow each balloon to go progressively higher than the one before it. Next envision the balloons in your right hand and repeat the exercise. You are balancing the chemistry in your brain and your chakras.

Joan's Meditation

Get into a comfortable position, sitting up or lying down on the floor, and make sure that your body is perfectly aligned. Place your hands on your knees (or by your side if you are lying down) with your palms up. If you can't sit or lay down on the floor, sit in a straight back chair with your body aligned and your feet flat on the floor.

Relax, breathing easily and place your hands on your Root Chakra. Place your hands on each chakra as we move from one chakra to the next up your body.

Think of the color red. Thank the Root Chakra for providing you the energy to succeed in whatever you undertake. Ask it to join the next chakra, the Sacral Chakra.

Think of the color orange. Thank the Sacral Chakra for providing you the ability to relate to others in a positive way. Ask it to join with the Root Chakra and go to the Solar Plexus Chakra.

Think of the color yellow. Thank the Solar Plexus Chakra for providing you personal power and the ability for psychic development. Ask it to join the first two chakras to go to the Heart Chakra.

Think of the color green. Thank the Heart Chakra for providing you unconditional love to love yourself and others. Ask it to join the first three chakras and go to the Throat Chakra.

Think of the color blue. Thank the Throat Chakra for providing you creativity and the possibility of transformation and healing, releasing anger. Ask it to join the other four chakras and go to the sixth chakra – The Third Eye.

Think of the color indigo or dark blue. Thank the Third Eye Chakra for providing you assistance in the letting go of negative tendencies and the elimination of selfish attitudes. Thank it also for guidance in tuning into your higher power. Ask it to join the other five chakras and go to the Crown Chakra.

Think of white or violet. Thank the Crown Chakra for providing you enlightenment, dynamic thought and the ability to connect with God.

Thank all the chakras for coming together, becoming one, in balance. Thank them for their blessings. Feel the connecting pure white light traveling from the bottom of your body to the top and from the top to the bottom of your body. Feel at ease and grateful knowing your body is working together in harmony. Relax in peace.

Chapter Thirteen: Your Own Practice Workbook

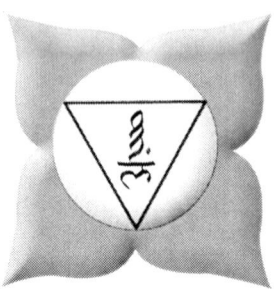

First Chakra – Root: located at the base of the spine at the tailbone in back, and the pubic bone in front. (Colors used: red, brown, black)

Root body parts: include hips, legs, lower back and sexual organs.

Blockage may make individual feel:

_____
_____
_____

Blockage may cause these problems:

_____
_____
_____

Gemstones: _____

Second Chakra – Belly: located 2 inches below the navel (Color used: orange.)

Root body parts: include women's sexual organs, kidneys, bladder and large intestine.

Blockage may make individual feel:

_____
_____
_____

Blockage may cause these problems:

_____
_____
_____

Gemstones: _____

THIRD CHAKRA – SOLAR PLEXUS: located 2 inches below the breastbone in the center behind the stomach (Color used: yellow)

Root body parts: include stomach, liver, gall bladder, pancreas and small intestine.

Blockage may make individual feel:
_____
_____
_____

Blockage may cause these problems:
_____
_____
_____

Gemstones:
_____

FOURTH CHAKRA – HEART: located behind breast bone in front and on the spine between the shoulder blades in back. (Color used: green and pink)

Root body parts: include heart, lungs, circulatory system, shoulders and upper back.

Blockage may make individual feel:
_____
_____
_____

Blockage may cause these problems:
_____
_____
_____

Gemstones: _____

Fifth Chakra – Throat: located in the V of the collarbone at the lower neck. (Color used: light blue)

Root body parts: include the throat.

Blockage may make individual feel:

_____
_____
_____

Blockage may cause these problems:

_____
_____
_____

Gemstones: _____

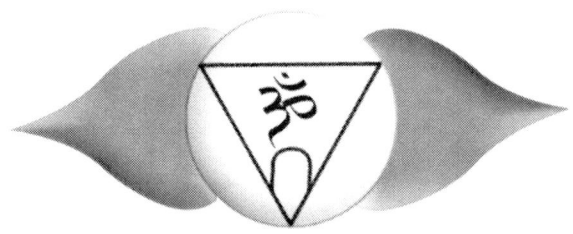

SIXTH CHAKRA – THIRD EYE: located above the physical eyes on the center of the forehead. (Colors used: purple and dark blue)
Root body parts: include eyes, face, brain, lymphatic and endocrine system.

Blockage may make individual feel:

_____
_____
_____

Blockage may cause these problems:

_____
_____
_____

Gemstones:
_____

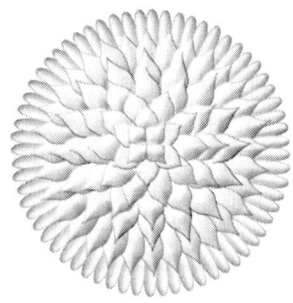

SEVENTH CHAKRA – CROWN: located just behind the top of the skull. (Colors used: white and purple)
Root body parts: include stomach, liver, gall bladder, pancreas and small intestine.

Blockage may make individual feel:

_____
_____
_____

Blockage may cause these problems:

_____
_____
_____

Gemstones:

_____

Bibliography and Recommended Reading

1. *Healing with Crystals and Chakra Energies* by Sue and Simon Lilly

2. *The Essential Crystal Handbook* by Simon and Sue Lilly

3. *The Chakra Bible* by Patricia Mercer

4. *Wheels of Life* by Anodea Judith

5. Website www.neatstuff.net/avalon

6. Website www.home.comcast.net

7. Website http://iffetsyoga.blogspot.com

8. Website www.crystalinks.com

9. Website www.chakra-balance.com

10. Website www.rapunzelgifts.com

11. Website www.feedback.nildram.co.uk/richarddebbs

12. Website www.kripalu.org

13. Website www.colourtherapyhealing.com

14. Website www.project-meditation.org

Notes

Notes

Notes

Notes

About the Author

Joan was born and raised in Elmira, New York, a small, farm city near the Pennsylvania border also known as the glider capital of the world. She and her twin sister and their older brother were raised in the soft times of the 1950s and followed the traditions of that era. After graduating from college, Joan married and had three children, becoming a single, working parent in the process. Several years later, she and her son moved to Ridgefield, Connecticut where she earned her Series 7 and worked as a Discount Stock Broker in a small, startup company in Stamford, Connecticut and New York City.

After two years, she moved to Boston, worked for a small, international insurance company and returned to school to graduate from Newbury College with an Associates Degree in Business Administration and Accounting. She then joined four other colleagues to form NiiS, a startup international insurance services company and worked for 10 years as its Director of Operations. In addition to overseeing the HR department, one of the areas of her expertise was telecommunications. Joan left NiiS in 1998 to accept an offer at Coastal Telecommunications, Inc. to help the company grow and served as its Executive Vice President. Then, in 2003, wanting to expand their business even more, Joan moved to Las Vegas, where she currently lives, and serves as President and co-owner in their company, Canyon Telecommunications, Inc.

At an early age, Joan had a near death experience and became aware of the "other side." All during her life, she has been interested in New Age beliefs and has studied with different groups to seek more knowledge. She believes that we are all one and one with our higher power, whoever that is for each of us; that God is loving and forgiving; that we are never alone;

that he is there for each one of us; that life is eternal. It is this strong belief on her part that allowed her to be at peace when her son, Jay, died of a drug overdose at Christmas in 2005. His death only increased her desire to become involved in the world of healing.

Joan believes we need to share whatever positive knowledge we have with others if it helps them spiritually better themselves whether it be mind, body or soul. One of the ways, she believes that she can make a difference and help others is by explaining in simplistic terms the jewels of our bodies, the seven main chakras, representing all the colors of the rainbow. If those seven chakras are in alignment, it opens up the opportunity to commune with our higher power, finding peace and better health. Joan's workshop empowers each individual to take control of their bodies to be as healthy as they can be through their chakras. Her strategies are simple and effective.

Her book, *The Seven Major Chakras – Keeping it Simple* is an easy guide to use as a reference for understanding the chakras and how to use this information and crystals to heal.

CPSIA information can be obtained at www.ICGtesting.com
Printed in the USA
BVOW012317041111

275334BV00004B/5/P